BADASS

DAD

for every man who is or desires to be the best dad on the planet

ERIC ROBERTSON

DEDICATION

This book is dedicated to my own father, who has overcome many of the negative consequences of his own childhood and has transformed himself into being an awesome dad. You are badass!

CONTENTS

CHAPTER ONE

I Said "Badass" Not "Jackass"

I will never forget it as long as I live.

Even if my dad doesn't recall it, perhaps conveniently, I do.

Even if my mother has wiped this pivotal and crucial moment from her memory, the imprint of this recollection still lives on in my head.

(Before I get started, it should be made known that my dad has done a lot of changing over the years. He has gone from decent to awesome over the last several years. And, when this happens, one must first step up and recognize not only the hellacious effort, but also the even more incredible result. It's not every day that people make leaps-and-bounds differences in their lives, but my father has done just that, so I first want to honor that and give him the ever-coveted title of "Badass Dad". He deserves it.)

But, none of us are perfect. And, not all of us were badass dads when we first started down this journey called fatherhood.

Most of us *(all of us, probably)* have had major struggles in being everything we wanted to be as a father. Before we had children, we felt that we would be the absolute best, baddest and awesomest kick-ass dads the world has ever known.

And we all have incidents in our lives where we know that, for the most part, we haven't really lived up to the hype we have been telling ourselves since the day we vowed to "never be like that" or "never to do that." *Not so badass.*

My father is no exception to this seemingly inevitable part of being a father, or just being a person. We all fall embarrassingly flat on our faces...and it sucks.

One such incident happened to me when I was just a child, probably 9-10 years old.

I grew up on a small farm and was handed the chore of mowing the lawn.

Now, you must understand that I had no ordinary lawn. It was a massive lawn and literally took 3 straight days to mow, and I had to mow it every week.

One bright Saturday morning, I had begun my weekly chore. I mounted our little Toro mower and started the long and seemingly endless task of mowing our grass. After a few hours (when I said 3 days, I meant 3 full, eight-to-ten-hour days) it was time for lunch. My mother sent out the message and I happily called it quits for a few minutes.

I turned off the blades, lifted the mowing deck and headed towards the garage to park the mower. My dad was in the garage and also heard the call to eat.

As I headed his way and he mine, he looked very disturbed, but by what I couldn't imagine. As far as I could tell, I hadn't done anything wrong. It had to have been one of my siblings who had crossed the line and was in for a verbal assault and reprimand.

Eric Robertson

I was wrong.

He was headed straight for me, and he wasn't getting any happier...which is weird, because I tend to think that everyone gets a little cheerier the closer they are to me.

As he approached me *(remember, I am only **9 or 10**)*, he raised up his foot and commenced to kick the crap out of that mower, rocking it nearly onto its two left wheels as I am sitting on top of it.

I am completely and utterly shocked.
I have no idea what is going on.
And, I may have pissed my pants a little.
"What did I do wrong?" I wondered.

Well, that question got answered, and the good part is I didn't even have to ask!!! He was more than eager to fill me in on my grievous transgression.

"You **JACKASS!**" he yelled. "You could have mowed a whole 'nother swath of grass on the way to the garage, but you shut off the mower..."

He then muttered something about wasted time. I don't quite recall. It was many years ago, and to be honest, I was still a little in shock over what had just happened.

But, I am sure of one thing: I was **not** the jackass that day. No, that title belonged to nonother than my father. Place the blue ribbon upon his chest.

You see, many men *(perhaps you are in this group...I hope not)* think that what it means to be a great, in charge, badass dad is to transform into some sort of monstrosity of a man. In our efforts to be the best dad we can be, we find ourselves falling incredibly short in the "badass department" and, unfortunately, we find ourselves being unbelievably adept in the "jackass department."

BUT I DIDN'T SAY JACKASS...I SAID BADASS!

Like I said earlier, none of us are perfect. I am, by far, not. When I talk to my wife, I have stories where I too have just been a big jackass-dad.

But I hope he remembers that in that moment, the best way to stop being a jackass is to be a badass. I hope he remembers to hold his kids in his arms and tell them he is sorry. I hope you will do the same.

It isn't too late, you know. It isn't too late to do the right thing for your kids. If they are young, go to their room and tell them how sorry you are.

Put this damn book down and do it right now.

If they are older, go see them. If they live far away, take a plane. If they won't see you, video call them. If they won't talk to you, send them an email or a letter. Do whatever it takes.

Because you don't want to be a jackass dad.
You want to be a Badass Dad.
And if you do what I just said...well, that is **BADASS**.

CHAPTER TWO

I Said "Badass" Not "Kiss Ass"

One of my best friends growing up was a kid named Peter Matthews. You could call him a neighbor, but where I grew up, neighbors were basically anyone that lived within a two-mile radius of your home.

He and I did pretty much everything together. We would spend hours playing football in his front yard, playing video games or hanging out at the local community pool in desperate attempts to get girls to notice us. It didn't work, but that didn't stop us from making every effort.

And, whenever we wanted to do something that for some might have been cost prohibitive (which for me growing up was pretty much everything), I knew I could count on Peter to make it happen. All he had to do was tell his dad (notice "tell", not "ask") what he was going to do and that it was going to cost "x" amount of dollars. His father, without hesitation, would immediately reach into his wallet and hand Peter whatever he asked for.

His dad might crack a joke like, "You are going to break me, son." Or, "Let me call the bank to see about getting a loan", but they were just jokes. Peter got what we needed. Every. Single. Time.

His dad was a kiss ass. Completely and totally. He didn't know what else to do.

You see, Peter lived almost his entire life without a mom. She had died tragically in an accident when he was just a few months old. And his dad had no idea what to do.

He wasn't prepared for this.
This isn't what he had imagined when they gave birth to their only son.
This wasn't the way life was supposed to be.

His wife was supposed to be there with him and for their child. That was the plan all along, but sometimes life happens and we are left without very many good options before us.

Long story short, his dad wasn't exactly sure how to be a single dad. So, he did what may have seemed like the right thing to do: make your kids happy by any means necessary.

I still remember (and I am a middle-aged man now) this one night in high school, as my friend and I stayed up entirely too late talking, the words that he spoke to me.

You see, Peter often wanted to go do things at very odd times of the night, or in places that were fairly far from home, and my parents simply would not allow me to go.

On this night, Peter wanted to go out on a school night to see a movie at the midnight showing. Of course, his dad was all for it, but my parents were not. They had these things called rules and boundaries that constantly kept me in balance. Peter wasn't going to go alone, so he didn't go.

My rules were the only rules he had.

And these are the words that he spoke to me that night as we weren't going to the movies: "I wish my dad loved me enough to give me rules."

Peter may have been spoiled rotten. His dad, somewhat understandably, may have kissed his ass at every crazy request, but Peter was no dummy.

He was able to stand on the outside and look into my family life and see, remarkably since he was only 16, that limits = love. Parameters meant Good Parenting. And he knew that his dad was doing it all wrong.

In life, I am a huge goofball and I rarely act my age, but in situation like this, I have always, for whatever reason, been an adult on this inside.

I told Peter that, first of all, he was nuts. His dad loved him more than anything in this life. He didn't kiss his ass because he doesn't love him; e kisses his ass because he does love him.

It wasn't a lack of love that made him a kiss ass.
It was a lack of knowledge.

His dad simply didn't know how to do it. His plans for family was thrown one of the worst curveballs life can throw, and he wasn't ready for it. Can anyone be "ready" for something like this?

No, but hopefully we do the best we can.

His dad may not have been badass, but at least he kept swinging at the curveball.
He never once gave up on his son.
He never once turned over his child for others to care for.

He was there, swinging as hard as he could. His only problem was that no one ever showed him how to

Eric Robertson

hold the bat, read the ball and swing. He was making it up as he went.

It has been decades since I have talked to Peter or his father. Time has caused us to drift apart and lose contact. But I often think of them and pray that they are well. And I hope that Peter remembers the words he spoke to me as he raised his own children, "limits = love".

The question we must deal with is this: are we badass dads or kiss ass dads?

My friend's dad had an excuse, or at least an understandable explanation as to why he did what he did.

More than likely you do not.

Many dads become kiss ass fathers because it is the easiest way to go. Give them what they want and they'll shut up, at least for a while.

But you bought this book, or it was given to you for a reason.

It was either given to you because someone, perhaps a child, thinks that you are a badass dad.
Or, because they wish that you would be.

Or you bought it in hopes of being the best dad you can possibly be.

In the end, it doesn't really matter if we have become the dad that gives in all the time because of tragic life events or because we are simply too lazy to give it our all. The end result is the same.

Regardless of the reason why we do what we do, kiss ass dads produce children who think that their parents don't love them. In turn, these kids grow up and possibly repeat the pattern that was set for them.

But this cycle has to end.

Being a great father isn't going to be easy.

Bending over backwards so that your kids can have everything they want might make them shut up, but it will also make them feel unloved and probably make them into not-so-great parents when they are older.

Think about it; what kind of dad would let their kids run the show? This is not badass.

Children need parents to set boundaries and create stability and order. Children don't know how to do this. Children will inevitably create chaos and disorder.

Boundaries are one of the best ways a parent can let their kids know just how important they are. Saying, "no" to your child is a great way to say "I love you."

So, are you a kiss ass dad or a badass dad?

If your kids are running the house, then it is time to set some boundaries, and quick. Otherwise, you will be living with little tyrants and dictators. Nobody wants that.

I am tempted at this point to give you some examples of what boundaries you should set, but I am hopeful that since you are actually reading this book, you have a functioning brain and that you already know what to do.

Unlike my friend's dad, you don't lack knowledge. You lack courage and will. There is no amount of words that I can put on a page that will ever give you that. This is something that has to well-up from the inside of you. This is something that you have to desire for yourself and your family.

You already know that they can't eat donuts before bed.

You already know that they can't wear their dirty clothes to school.

You already know that talking to their boy/girlfriend until 2am is wrong.

You are not an idiot!

But you might be a coward. A really knowledgeable coward.

FYI...this is not badass. Not even close.

So, to all the dads that need to kick their own ass into gear: do it. Be a badass without becoming a jackass. Take control of your family's situation before you simply cannot. If your kids are grown, apologize for the mistakes you made and hope to God they will not do what you did.

Another FYI...if you do this, your kids will automatically put you into the badass-dad ranking.

And, for all you dads that have been setting boundaries and love-limits for your kids: keep it up. They may act like they hate you *(not much worse than having a kid tell you they do),* but trust me.

THEY DON'T! Keep on doing it. Don't get lazy. Don't grow weary. You've got to get up every day and make a new determination to be the dad your kids need you to be.

Now that is badass.

CHAPTER THREE

Badass Dads Are There

It is an easy trap to fall into as a dad.

We work our asses off and struggle to make ends meet.

We put up with situations and spend endless hours with people we would maybe otherwise never even talk to just to give our families what they need.

Our supervisor sucks, but we can't say or do anything because we love our family.

Our hours are atrocious, but what can a dad do? There are mouths to feed, bills to pay, insurances to provide and, well, those people in your house can't walk around naked and shoeless. And you are most likely sharing these responsibilities with your wife, or perhaps you are doing it alone.

Either way, it isn't easy. The everyday tasks of life can be a major drain on our emotions, sapping us of our energy and often, in our mid-40s, leading us to question everything we have ever done in life.

I have known too many men, who at this age and stage in life, decided that they have had enough.

They turn tail and run.

They were on the path to being a badass dad, but instead turned into a punk-ass wannabe-teenage boy who would rather spend all their money on sports cars and spoiling a "younger lady" in a desperate attempt to feel young, vibrant and alive again than be there for their family.

Now, many men will say that what they do in their married life has no effect on how they are as a dad. "I can be a bad husband and a good father."

Look, I am not saying that, to be a good father, your marriage has to work out. If that is what you read, I want you to read this again.

I am saying that, to be a badass dad, you can't be a punk-ass husband. You need to be there.

Great dads (hopefully you fit this description) don't give in to the crazy thoughts spurred on by our "last blast" of testosterone before we take the downhill plunge into getting old. We don't let our emotions get overwhelmed by the feelings that seem to wash over us like a wave when we feel underappreciated, unloved and disrespected.

Great dads deal with it. We wrestle our emotions to the ground and remind ourselves of what we really want in life.

Badass dads are there. And they stay there!

I know of one family in particular who is currently suffering under the harmful abandonment of a punk-ass dad.
(actually, even putting the word "dad" at the end seems too respectful)

This man has a 13-year-old son and a 7-year-old daughter. A little over a year ago, this "man" decided that he wasn't ready for all this father/husband stuff.

He walked out on his entire family.

He didn't just leave his wife. That would have been bad enough, but not every marriage is meant to be. He could have simply got an apartment close by and agreed to at least partner with the mom in raising their kids.

This isn't what he did. Like so many, he fled the scene of the family altogether. He moved away to a completely different state and has never been seen or heard of since.

Like I said, he isn't a badass. He is a punk-ass and I pray to God that he changes his attitude and actions before his son grows up and thinks that this is what you do when things get tough. Before he thinks that it is okay to give in to our all-too-often natural impulse to run and never show up again.

BADASS DAD

I hope his little girl gets to have her dad in her life before she gets older and has to deal with the issues of thinking that her dad doesn't love her...and that it is all her fault.

And I pray, I really pray, that he turns his boat around before he has drifted so far out to sea that he doesn't even know how to get back to the dry land of his family that he once was there for.

He will miss every game of soccer, basketball his son will ever play.
He will be painfully absent from every princess birthday party his daughter ever has.
His son will go on his first date, but he won't be there to tell him how to properly treat one of the most precious creatures God ever created.
His daughter will get married, hopefully to a man who will turn out to be a badass dad, but he won't be there to give her away.

One day there may be so much emotional distance between them that he will never find his way back into their hearts and lives. And he will have to live the rest of his life knowing that his loneliness and pain have come from the self-inflicted wounds of the actions he took in moments of weakness and selfishness.

Our actions as men have a major influence on the lives of our kids, old and young.

One of the most painful things a child can remember, aside from the tragedy of abuse, is remembering all the times that dad wasn't there.

They remember that time they scanned through the stadium, looking to see if dad was there to see their first cheer or first goal, only to see mom sitting alone.

They remember, as they stood as part of a quartet or choir, and looked to see if dad really did make it to see the concert, only to see their mother sitting next to strangers and parents of classmates.

This is a crime against children. You may not be able to make it to every event, and that is fine. Actually, it is more than fine. Kids need to know that, while you love them with all your heart, they are not the center of the universe. But never, or hardly ever being there *(or being there with a scowl on your face because your wife made you go)* is far from badass. It is pathetic and if reading this makes you feel like a piece-of-crap-father, then GOOD!

But don't just sit there. People can change.

YOU can change.

You may not be the father you have always wanted to be. You may not have been there when your children needed you. You may have been a total flake of a father.

As long as you have breath in your lungs, you have hope.

The journey back to your family will be scary. You will have to man-up and face the fact that they may not want you. You may have to deal with utter rejection at the hands of the children you rejected. Accept it. Deal with it. You made a mess, so don't expect everything to be nice and tidy when you get back.

You are going to have to stand in the face of your deepest fears and past failures, look them in the eye, and tell them that you are not going to be guided and led by them any longer. You have made a decision, a *determination*, to make things as right as you can make them.

This is badass!

Even if your kids never let you back in their lives, you know that you are headed down the path that you chose, not out of selfishness and despair, but out of love. And your kids will know, especially if you never quit doing what is right, that you are a man on a mission to become the best man you can be.

Who knows? They may one day slowly open the door of their lives to you. Either way, you are going to keep going and be all you were created to be. At the very least, you will be an example to them of just what a man can do when they have made up their minds to make needed changes and start (and finish) the journey towards greatness. The journey alone is worth the effort.

To those dads who were there, I want to send out a sincere "thanks".

You treated their mother with respect and love every day, even though you might not have been together anymore.

You worked those long hours, went through hell and came back every day to make sure your children knew they were one of the most important parts of your life.

You managed to navigate the tumultuous waters of the midlife crisis and came out the other side, perhaps without a sports car, but with your pride as a man healthily intact.

You were there to show your son how to open a door for his prom date.

You were there to show him how to have a difficult but needed conversation with his wife when they don't see eye to eye.

You were there to show your daughter what kind of man they should be looking for when they decide they want to give their life in marriage to another.

You were there, sitting in the audience, as your children scanned to auditorium to find you in hopes of flashing you a big, beautiful smile during their concert.

You were there, after the game was over, to show your son the picture you took as he shot the final goal in the game.

You were there as your daughter made the winning shot of her high school basketball game.

You were there at the hospital with them when their appendix decided it needed to be removed.

You were there. You were there. You were there.

And that is badass.

CHAPTER FOUR

Badass Dads Are Selfless

This is a tough description.

I mean, who is truly selfless anyway? And, can you ever get to the point where you can honestly say to yourself, "I am not self-serving. I put the needs of others, especially my family, before my own. I have arrived...and am humble too."?

None-the-less, being a great father is going to mean just this. It is going to mean, in a variety of different ways, that the needs of your children are more important than your own personal ambitions and wants.

Now, moms tend to do this naturally. I see this tendency in my wife nearly every day, in big and small ways.

When my parents would come to visit, she asked that they stay with us for at least 4 weeks. In our house.

We moved beds around.

We used to share our own bed with our youngest one for weeks straight (you guessed it: marital bliss was put on hold).

My wife would literally cook 3 meals a day for EVERYONE just so my parents could be with us.

And she did it for the kids. She wanted our children to have a relationship with my parents and she was willing to pay nearly any price and suffer major changes within our household to make it happen.

Let's be honest: does anyone really ever "want" to cook that much?

Does anyone ever desire to be cramped for over one month, sharing bathrooms and laundry days?

No. No one.

But, my wife was (and still is) selfless. There isn't a need she has that is more important than the needs of our children.

There isn't a desire she has ever had that outweighed the love and importance of the wants and desires of our own children. And she would nearly sacrifice anything to make sure they have what they want and need.

I remember the BC years of our marriage (you know, Before Children) when my wife would go to her favorite clothing stores and buy herself whatever she wanted.

Eric Robertson

The best and most stylish shoes. Done.

The most beautiful dresses. Easy.

The latest trends in clothing and apparel. Taken care of.

But, as soon as our first child opened her eyes and let out her first cry, my wife did what I thought to be impossible.

And, she didn't even have to try.

Without hesitation, and seemingly without thought, every desire she once had to own the best things and wear the best clothes immediately got transferred to our daughter. This transition seemed only natural to her.

And this trend continued with our second child, our son, and our third child, our youngest daughter.

I do not remember the last time my wife went to and purchased for herself something that she *really wanted*.

And, it isn't the case that she stopped wanting things for herself.

It is just that my wife understood, and understands, that part of what it means to be a great parent is to put the needs of your children above your own wants.

If you want to be a badass dad, then you are going to need to take a page out of her book.

This isn't going to be easy.

Men, by nature, are not selfless. When my kids were born, I didn't have the same, intuitive, natural and immediate switch from "me-centered" to "them-centered". I had to work at it. Fortunately for me, I had a great example in my life to help me do that (though, I must admit that my wife may have gotten too carried away with it, and I was there to help balance her selflessness just as she helped to balance my selfishness).

It is time to take a mental (or physical, if needed) inventory of where your life is spent.

I have known men who seemed to never have enough money for a small family vacation, but the fridge was always full of beer and the smokes never seemed to fall short.

I have known men who never seemed to have two dimes to rub together when it came to activities for the kids (soccer, choir, football or theater), but who never failed to play poker every

Friday or go to the bar for drinks after work to "unwind" from the stresses of life.

Hopefully none of what I am saying describes you, but I have known men who simply have no time for their children, but who always seem to have time for themselves.

There is still time to watch the game.
There is still time to go hang with the boys.
There is still time to go target shooting with friends.
There is still time to tinker with the new toy that now sits in the garage, gloriously waiting to be fixed and running.
BUT there isn't any time for the kids.

If you have been this kind of dad, then it goes without saying that you are not a badass dad.

You are selfish.

You put yourself first, always.

And you can't hide behind the rhetoric of, "I pay the bills and put food on the table!" As important as this is, it is only part of what a badass dad does.

Your children do not live on bread alone.
They need YOU!

They need to see you at most of their games.
They need to know that they are more important that poker night or buddy time.

They need to feel it, deep down and hopefully while they are still young, that their father *(that's YOU)* values them enough to put their needs above your own.

This doesn't mean "no more happiness."

This doesn't mean "no more friends, beer or poker."

It simply means that you are going to need to balance your own needs and desires with the needs and desires of your children.

You may need to use a vacation day to spend it with your kids on their birthdays.

You may need to miss poker (and be happy about it) because that child you love so much has a band concert (and you hate band) that same night. You don't like band, but you LOVE your child and there isn't a game, friend or drink in the world that will dissuade you from going.

And, here is the coolest thing:

Badass dads share their joys with their kids!

That car, that new toy I referred that is in your garage, that needs to be fixed can be with the help of your children. Make them a part of what makes you happy. They may slow you down, but the point isn't that the car is fixed and running as fast as possible. The point is that you did it together.

And games? What child doesn't love to play games. Teach your son or daughter how to play your favorite card game.

You don't always need to sacrifice your passion. You just need to share it.

Most moms do this naturally.

Most men need to work at it.

But it is a work that is worth doing.

If you are a dad and this has been the way you parent, congratulations. You are one of the best, baddest and most impressive dads on the planet. Your kids are going to be better off for it and the world is going to be a better place because of it.

If you have read this chapter and thought, "I am not this way at all, or at least not enough", then it is time you make a change. And it doesn't matter if your kids are 4 or 40! Make a change.

As stated previously, not every adult child is going to accept "the new you" you have decided to be.

You are going to have to be okay with that.

Because, hopefully at some point, they will see that you, like my own father, are making every effort to become a badass dad...even if it means becoming a badass grandad.

And as much as they might wish you had been this selfless for them, they will hopefully let you be selfless for their own kids.

Perhaps you are the son or daughter with a parent who has been struggling to be a better one, but you are refusing to let them. I've got news for you; you are not being badass. You are being selfish. It is time to change.[1]

Your kids deserve to have a grandfather or grandmother in their lives. Even if they weren't

---

[1] I recognize that in some cases, allowing your bad parent access to your own children can be harmful and dangerous. I am not here talking about allowing God-awful parents, abusers or manipulators back into your lives. That would be stupid. I am talking about parents who perhaps haven't been the greatest and are genuinely working to fix it. Only you know your situation. Just make sure your decision is being made based on the needs of your kids, not a selfish desire to not deal with your parents any more.

the greatest in your own life, they can be great in the life of your children.

Be selfless.

Let them!

Why?

Because badass dads are selfless. That's why.

CHAPTER FIVE

Badass Means Mentor

I am not an athletically inclined person.

I wasn't born with the ability to throw, run, catch or really do any other number of things most athletes do. I do exercise and lift to stay in shape, but just don't expect me to do a triathlon or play a game of pick up with the other dads at the park.

Actually, I will play, but usually when I am done the other players are wishing I had just stayed on the sidelines.

No, my childhood was filled with other sorts of activities, none of which would ever equate to "manliness" in any sense of the word. Well, at least it didn't in the years I was a child.

I spent my days singing in choirs, show choirs, doing theater and generally setting myself up as the least desirable boy in school. But, I loved it (still do), so I did it anyway. I wasn't about to stop doing what I loved just because it made me an easy target for jokes.

No, I did what I loved and often thought that if I ever had a son (if some girl was every lucky enough to catch me...) I would be able to teach him about singing, harmonies, proper stage placement and the like.

As luck would have it, I did have a son. He is a wonderful son who, in fact, does love to sing and dance. It looked like I was going to be able to do fill my heart's desire.

I imagined sitting down with him and teaching him the basics of music theory, how to hear harmony and how to sing clearly with proper breathing. I was going to be his vocal coach!

Except that when it came time to get involved in some sort of afterschool activity, he selected football. And, it appears that he could only think of one person whom he thought was best suited to teach him all the ins-and-outs of football. That person was me. At least in his head, it was me. I mean, why wouldn't it be me, right?

Every other coach was a dad, and he wanted his dad to be one too.

Only one problem: I didn't know a damn thing about football. Not when it came to playing the game anyway. I understood the rules. I understood the basics. (I'm not an idiot about sports, I just don't like them. Though, most people upon hearing one "doesn't like sports" immediately thinks they are utterly stupid about sports and then proceeds to treat them as such.

Its maddening, but I digress...) But I had never played.

I didn't know how to throw a ball correctly.

I didn't know how to properly catch a football.

Least of all, I wasn't (and am still not, in fact) used to helping anyone physically hit another person. We didn't do that in choir.

None of this mattered to my son. I was his dad, and his dad could do anything.

His dad could kickass.

His dad could throw a perfect spiral with impeccable accuracy.

His dad could always make the winning catch and run the ball down the field into the end zone.

His dad was awesome.

The only problem was, as you have already rightly guessed, I am not awesome. Not at sports anyway.

Who was I to mentor my kid, or any kid for that matter, on a sport I couldn't play? I had to make a choice. It wasn't an easy choice. I mean, I may not be athletic, but I had no desire to embarrass myself or my kid. My pride in self and family was still firmly intact.

In the end, I did approach the coaching staff and informed them that I would like to participate as a "coach" of some sort. I was upfront with them about my complete lack of experience, knowledge and ability in this arena. They accepted me. It was weird, but they did.

I then started the task of trying to appreciate and learn about a game that I had otherwise had no interest in whatsoever. I learned the rules. I practiced with the kids.

In fact, after having thrown a horrible pass to a ref during a game (It was truly atrocious. Think "handicapped duck attempting flight" type of pass) the ref looked at me in astonishment that a coach could be so awful. It wasn't cool.

I remember the head coach actually pulled me aside and said, "Has no one ever showed you how to throw a ball?"

"No...no one ever has. And I never asked."

He spent the next 30 minutes trying to give me the basics of proper form and technique. And, after some practice, it worked! Even for a guy like me.

My son wanted a mentor. He wanted his dad to be there, teach him and show him the way.

And I had to let go of my pride and learn a game I had no interest in so that I could be there for my son.

I think this is part of what it means to be a badass dad. You become selfless and humble. You put the needs of your children over the petty thoughts of ego and self-centeredness.

I had to put aside time, not only for coaching and games, but also time to learn the game myself. And I did it for him.

In the end, I didn't want to be a dad that sat on the sidelines and hid behind the façade of "I'm not an athlete". I didn't have time to waste with excuses like, "I don't know the game".

Our kids need us to step up to the plate and be there for them. Maybe that means you need to learn a little something about music because your son or daughter has a passion for playing piano or guitar. You may never learn enough to teach them everything they need to know, but you can learn enough to let them know you are genuinely interested in what they love.

Many of you have done just this. You stepped up when your kids needed you and gave them your time and mentorship, at least as long as you could. I think they will remember this. I believe moments like these can change their lives forever. When they are older and you are perhaps gone, they will look back and know that their father loved them so much that he actually learned something new, just for them.

My son does. I remind him of this from time to time. He needs to remember because, when he has kids, he needs to remember the pattern that I set for him and copy it.

It is time to let go of our egos and pride. It is time to let go of our fears of failure. Maybe it is time to just simply stop being a selfish jerk and to start putting your children's needs over your own desires and wants.

You do have time! If my former boss, owner of a multimillion dollar company had time to coach his son's baseball team (my boss knew nothing about baseball), then you do to.

You can learn, at least up to a point.

Otherwise, your children run the risk of thinking that dad simply doesn't care about what they are passionate about. Or worse, dad not only does not care, he doesn't even want to care.

I want my children to know that I am passionate about them, even when they are passionate about making YouTube videos...something I care very little about, except that they care A LOT about it!

I want my kids to know that, while I may not become a master of their trade or skill, I am interested enough to learn something. And, if they are young, I am interested enough in it to teach them what I do know, and even learn more so that I have more to share.

Living as a dad, in this way, takes effort. It won't happen naturally for most people. You are going to have to make a decision to be a mentor to your kids.

This is a decision that many of you have already made. This decision and execution is totally badass. You are to be acknowledged as one of the best dads on the planet.

This is a decision that you can still make. Know your kids. Know their passion. Take some initiative and let them know you care. You never know, not only will you learn something, you might even gain some insights that you can share.

Make the choice to be a great dad.
Make the decision to be badass

CHAPTER SIX

Badass Means Love

Love.

It was a word scarcely used in my house as a child.

Now, I am sure that my father told me multiple times, when I was very young and it was very easy, that he loved me.

He probably tickled me, rolled around on the floor with me, threw me in the air and ended each activity with a flurry of goofy, "I love YOU!" type statements.

If he did, I am glad he did. And, if I could change one thing about my childhood, it would simply be this: I wish he had continued telling me he loved me.

I have no childhood memories of him telling me. I don't remember him ever hugging me on my birthday. I have no recollection of him patting me on the back and telling me how proud he was.

Most of my childhood memories of my dad are of him working out in the garage, trying to keep the cars running so he could get to work. We didn't have money for mechanics, so he took it upon himself to make sure things were taken care of. After working some long, grueling hours fixing roads and bridges and then coming home to fix vehicles, he didn't have much energy for anything else.

That included time with kids.

It isn't that my dad didn't love me and my siblings. He did. I am certain that he loved us a great deal. It is just that expressing love in any verbal way was never something we did.

His father didn't do it.

He didn't grow up with affection and warmth from his dad, so the thought of being that way probably seemed a little weird...or never even crossed his mind.

But, there did come a time when he decided to make a change. I remember it well, and my reaction, as you will soon see, was less than spectacular.

A lady from our church, a fairly new member and very opinionated (in a good way), had made friends with my family. She, unlike us, grew up in a very affectionate and huggie-feely family. She thought we were tons of fun to be around (she was right for thinking thus), but it didn't take her long to realize that we were about the least affectionate family she had ever been around.

I am sure that, in comparison with her own upbringing, our family must have felt like someone had reached in to the center of our familial emotions bank and withdrew every penny.

No hugs.
No "I love you".
No emotional conversations of any kind.

It probably felt more like a battalion than a family in this regard. A fun battalion, but still...a battalion.

She, wisely I might add, decided that something needed to be done about this horrible way of living.

And so, she began the grooming process. A process that would one day culminate in my father looking me in the eye and saying these words: "Son, I love you."

That day came, and it is as etched in my psyche as the day he called me a jackass. Completely unforgettable.

It happened one day as I was headed to the local grocery store to go to work. It was a normal day, like so many that had gone before. Except for those four words. They were words the words that I didn't even know I wanted to hear.

And, upon hearing these strange words in the voice of my father, I did the only natural thing I could think of.

"Uh, ok."

That was it. I proceeded to my car and went to work.

And then I spent the rest of my 8-hour shift wondering what the hell just happened.

I mean, it made no sense.

And it was so out of the blue.

There was no warm up. No prelude to a word of love. Just a (wonderfully) awkward moment. The awkwardness was doubled due to the fact that the lady from church was there when it happened. I am certain she was hoping to celebrate a successful mission of love.

Epic. Fail.

I have no idea what it took to make my father utter those seemingly forbidden words. How many days, weeks, months of her life were spent to convince him that this was the right thing to do? I haven't a clue.

All I know is that my response was, well, really bad.

In my defense, she hadn't been grooming me as she had been my father (probably thought she wouldn't need to). So, for the sake fairness, it is understandable as to why I wasn't really ready with a good comeback.

She quickly figured out that our whole family was messed up, not just my dad (and she had me to thank for this revelation). She met with me the next day personally and asked me what I thought of what my dad said. I think I told her I thought it was weird or something...I don't rightly recall. She then spent a few minutes with me, telling me how I hurt my father deeply with my response.

It may seem silly to you (or maybe it doesn't), but it took about as much courage as my dad could muster to say those words to me. And when I responded with only one real word ("uh" doesn't qualify), he was about to never say those words again. I know this because she told me that he said exactly that to her.

But, our friend was no quitter.

She actually told me, "I am going to have your dad try again. When he does, you should say 'I love you too, dad.' Okay?"

I agreed.

He did try again.

And he has never stopped trying since.

I remember weeping as a young man in my early 20s, wishing that the love we shared and spoke to one another as adults had been a part of my childhood.

But it wasn't.
And there isn't a damn thing that I or my father can do about it.

The only thing in our control is what happens now, what we do now, what we say now.

So, we have both grabbed to bull by the horns and are taking control of our lives.

There isn't a conversation that ends that doesn't end with an "I love you."

Every phone call ends the same way.

Every trip, as we eventually say our goodbyes, concludes with love.

Eric Robertson

If I ever wondered if my father loves me, those doubts have long faded into the past. I know he loves me. He tells me every time we talk.

And my response is, "I love you too, dad."

Children need to hear the words. They need to see acts of love and kindness; this is, of course, true. They need the hugs; my father and I hug often. They need the words also. The words, the hugs and the actions leave no doubt. They are loved.

For most of us, love doesn't come easy. When our kids are small and love to cuddle, it perhaps is.

But as they grow, expressions of love get harder.

As my oldest daughter got older, I actually found myself physically moving away from her. Like the lady at church, my wife noticed immediately. And, after some very thoughtful and kinds words, I corrected my direction. Because it isn't enough for the toddler version of my kids to hear the words and feel the embrace. The teen version, the college version and even the fully grown and on her own version needs to have this.

If you are a naturally loving father, I salute you. This does come easy to many and you should thank God that you are blessed with at least this great parenting skill.

If, however, you are anything like me, then showing your kids you love them is going to require work.

Being this kind of dad won't happen on its own.

You are going to have to make a decision and work at it.

You are going to have to decide that this is something that you want in your life and in the life of your kids and then pursue this goal with everything you have.

Well, at least at first. Love gets easier the more you do it. But you have to start. You have to make the effort and never give up.

Your love as a father will literally change the direction of your kids' life forever. Your lack of love will do the same. Only one direction is good though.

It is time to get your ass in gear. Your kids are only with you so long, and then they are gone. What memories will they carry with them?

Will their only memory be that of being called a jackass?

Will they only recall all the times you didn't play with them?

Will they only call to remembrance the lack of affection you gave them?

Or, will you muster up the courage and strength to change the kind of dad you are? I can't answer that, but you can. And you answer it you must!

Otherwise, you will be, perhaps, an "okay dad." That is if you are lucky! You may end up in the "lame-ass dad" bucket. Too lazy to make a change. Too self-centered to put your kids first. Too scared to love.

This is not badass. This is just bad.

But, for those of you who are loving, those of you who did the work, went against your natural tendency to distance yourselves from your kids, to you belongs the title of badass dad.

You aren't perfect. But this book isn't for the perfect dad or the man who wants to be perfect. It is for the man who is or will one day be badass. I hope that is you.

CHAPTER SEVEN

Surrounded by Badass Dads

Chances are, if you have ever accomplished anything noteworthy in your life, you didn't do it alone.

Think about it. Even the things in life that you now take for granted are the direct result of having other people in your life that have helped you along the way.

You didn't learn to talk all on your own. Maybe you never put much thought into this portion of your life, but if you hadn't had other people around you, you wouldn't even be able to communicate effectively.

You didn't learn to walk all by your little self.

You didn't learn to read, swim, drive, do math, act, sing, dance *(I'm still working on this one...probably a lost cause)* play sports or even eat without the help and influence of others.

Think about your line of work as an example.

Let's say you are in sales. If you work for an organization that is worth anything at all, they have invested time and resources into making you a great salesman. Sure, they do this for selfish reasons as they want you to sell as much product at the highest margin you can get. But they also do this because they know something: you can't be a great salesman alone. If you are going to be a major producer for them, then you are going to need training. You are going to need teachers, mentors and guidance from those who have already gone down that path.

It is this way in every area of life.

Teachers are constantly getting additional training from others in order to better themselves.

Construction workers habitually go through safety trainings to make sure that they are working as safe as possible (and to cover the ass of the company).

CEOs have special groups they meet with in order to achieve and perform at the highest level they are capable of.

What is more is the fact in every area of life, especially regarding finances, men (and woman, but this book is for dads) strive to do and achieve as much as possible.

It is a matter of pride for us to work hard, perform well, earn good wages and provide for our families.

Nothing wrong with that. It would be an embarrassment if you didn't care about taking care of your family. If this is you, just go back to the beginning of this book and start over.

The problem is that we often care deeply about being the best painter, preacher, teacher or leader in our industry, putting in time, money and energy to that end. But when it comes to being a dad, we frequently do nothing to make sure that happens.

When was the last time you went to a seminar on how to be a great dad?

When was the last time you go together with other dads in an effort to learn from one another, get great "dad-ideas" and truly better yourself?

It is entirely possible that you have never done any of the above. So, how about these:

When was the last time you called your own father (or whoever raised you) and asked them for advice?

Have you ever gone to your pastor at church and asked them for some counsel on raising kids?
(yes, I said church! don't knock it until you've tried it)

What books (besides this one) have you ever read to help give you parenting tips and skills so that you can be the best dad you are capable of being?

If you have answered no to ALL of these questions, go ahead and own it.

Don't sit there and explain to me (I can't hear you anyway) why you don't do those things.

"I can't call my dad. He sucked as a dad."

Well, that may very well be the case. Perhaps you dad wasn't really all that great. Maybe he didn't go to your games or concerts, or looked like he'd rather have been anywhere but there when he was present.

So what?

Give him a call. I bet he has some great advice on what *not to do*. Even mediocre dads have more experience than you and probably have a lot to offer if you'd only give them a chance.

If you dad was abusive, find the next best thing you had in your life as a father. Go and ask that guy.

It may very well be that when it comes to finding a great "father-pattern" to follow, you simply had no one in your life. You have no memories of great parenting to rely on and no one from your past to go to.

I encourage you to find someone. My former employer was an absolute badass dad and his kids grew up to be wonderful, kind, loving and reliable people. If my own father hadn't changed his life so much, I would have gone to him more than I did for help.

Notice I said "would have gone more".

I expanded my circle and got advice from multiple sources. I didn't only ask my dad. I asked other dads as well.

I surrounded myself with badasses.

As men, we need to take our role as fathers at least as seriously as we do our professional lives.

It is important to do well at work. Our children and families are counting on it. This is part of being a great father.

But they are also counting on us to know what to do, not just as a "father-provider", but just as a father.

Remember my friend Peter, who's dad basically let him do whatever he wanted because his dad simply had no idea what he was doing? That man should have surrounded himself with some other dads to help him along the way. But he didn't. And his son spent much of his life thinking his dad didn't love him.

There is going to come a time when your child is going to need to be punished, but the situation is also delicate. You are going to need help navigating the waters of discipline to make sure that your child learns the much-needed lesson but doesn't feel that the punishment came out of anger or was harsher than deserved. When moments like these arise, you need someone you can count on who has been there and done that.

There is going to come a time when your daughter comes home broken hearted and needs the love of a father to console and heal her. Your natural reaction may as mine once was: to retreat ever so slightly and let mom do the work.

But this is the wrong move. If you had a great dad you could turn to in moments like these, then these times of turmoil would be less worrisome.

The list of possible moments where you will need to be a great dad goes on and on. Pregnancies, breakups, bullying, pornography problems, lying, cheating, sneaking around...

Any of these things are almost bound to happen.

Surrounding yourself with badasses will make those moments more easily manageable. Being surrounded by people like this will make you the best dad you can possibly be.

As a side note, it is worth mentioning that I am not advocating that you try and be like these other men. I don't want people constantly comparing themselves to others. For whatever reason, some men are just more naturally gifted at fatherhood than others just like some are more naturally athletic than others.

When I seek advice and counsel from others, it isn't because I want to be just like them, but rather because I know that they may have guidance that is going to help **Me** be the **Best Me**. I am not trying to become them. Nor do I feel bad when they give me an idea and it is simply something I cannot do. This isn't a competition to see who the best dad is.

However, just getting the advice is a great way forward. Often, the ideas I received were ideas that I would never have thought of *(because I am not them)*. And, like advice on how to sell, build or teach, I modified those ideas to fit who I am.

Eric Robertson

We are not trying to be the best dad THEY can be.

We are attempting to be the best dad WE can be!

Will you take the role as father as seriously as you do the other areas of your life?

Will you invest the same time, energy and money into being a great dad as you do your professional life?

Will you even do something you haven't done in years? Will you go to church and find some men who have the similar goal of being the dad their families need them to be?

Will you surround yourself with great dads?

If so, or if you have already been doing just this, then I submit to you that you are, or are well on your way, to being a Badass Dad.

If you are reluctant, then you need to stop and think about why you are. What is stopping you from doing this or any of the other things mentioned in this book?

Is it selfishness? Do you not want to devote more time to being a better dad?

Is it fear? Are you afraid of what others might say if they know you need help?

Take a moment and think about it. I believe you can be a great dad. It isn't going to be easy. You are going to need some help. Everyone needs help for everything. Let go of your pride and be the dad I know you can be, the dad you want to be, the dad your family longs for you to be.

CHAPTER EIGHT

Are You Badass?

This book is dedicated to you.

It is dedicated to all of you dads who have devoted your lives to your children.

You were there at their games, concerts and school events, even when it required a sacrifice of time and perhaps even money.

You were there, involved in their lives, setting boundaries and giving the proper amount of discipline when it was needed.

You were badass enough to apologize to them when you realized that you had crossed the line between badass and jackass.

You knew and continue to know that being a great dad doesn't mean you never make a mistake, but it does mean owning up to your shortcomings and apologizing in humility.

You have taken the time to surround yourselves with great fathers in an effort to be the best dad you can be for your children.

If this describes you, then you are indeed a badass dad. If this book is a gift from a child of yours, you now know why they saw the book and thought of you. You, my friend, are a great dad and your kids know it and have honored you with this book. More importantly, they have honored you in their hearts by recognizing just how much your time, energy and love has positively affected their lives. Congratulations! You deserve their honor.

For everyone else, the challenge to be a great dad has been issued.

For those of you who one-day hope to be a dad, this book has provided you with real stories and really good advice on how to be the dad you say you want to be. The question has changed from "How can I be a great dad?" to "Will I put in the work and dedication it takes to be a great dad?"

Will you put as much effort in to being a dad as you do being a great salesman, construction worker or business owner?

How important is this goal of being a badass dad? Your actions will reveal to you just where this goal stands in relation to the other things you hope to achieve.

Will you avoid setting appointments on certain days so you can help coach a game you know little to nothing about?

Will you give the much needed tough-love when it would be easier to just give in and give them what they want?

Will you seek out counsel from others who have been down the road of fatherhood and know what you should do, especially when you don't know what to do? Will you ask for advice even when you think you DO know what to do (because sometimes you are wrong)?

You can do it! Your future will thank your past if you start now.

And, for those who haven't really been the dad you wanted to be to this point, it isn't too late to make a change. My dad did it late in life. You can do it too. At this point, the only obstacle prohibiting you from moving from mediocre (or just plain terrible) dad to badass dad is you. You are the only one in your way.

So, the question is: Are You Badass?

19439742R00066

Made in the USA
Middletown, DE
05 December 2018